1

ART NOUVEAU

ART NOUVEAU

JUGENDSTIL

STILE LIBERTY

ARTE NUEVO

アール・ヌーヴォー

藝術奇葩

ART NOUVEAU

DOVERPICTURA

DOVER PUBLICATIONS, Inc. | Mineola, New York

Selected and designed by Thalia Large and Alan Weller.

Art Nouveau is a new work, first published by Dover Publications, Inc., in 2004.

For permission to use more than ten images, please contact:
Permissions Department
Dover Publications, Inc.
31 East 2nd Street
Mineola, NY 11501
rights@doverpublications.com

The CD-ROM file names correspond to the images in the book. All of the artwork stored on the CD-ROM can be imported directly into a wide range of design and word-processing programs on either Windows or Macintosh platforms. No further installation is necessary.

International Standard Book Number: 0-486-99639-5

Manufactured in Hong Kong
Dover Publications, Inc., 31 East 2nd Street, Mineola, NY 11501
www.doverpublications.com

3

4

5

6

7

8

9

10

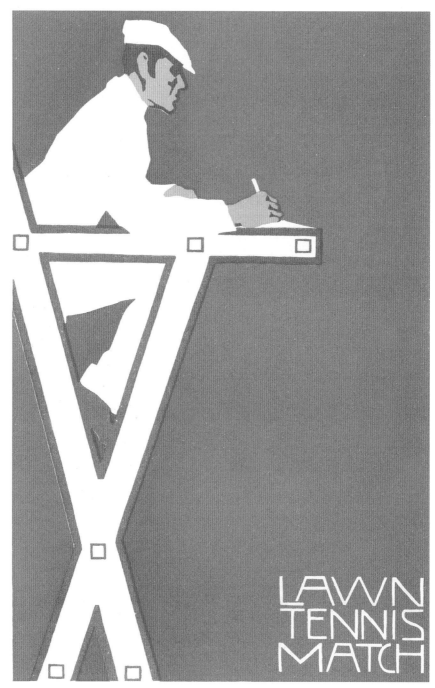

LAWN
TENNIS
MATCH

11

12

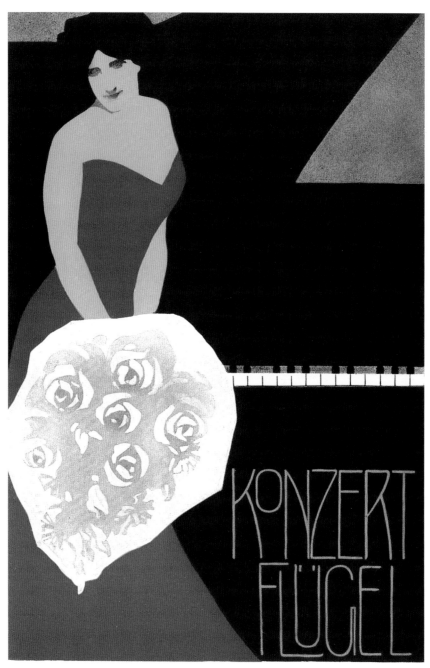

KONZERT
FLÜGEL

13

14

15

16

17

18

19

20

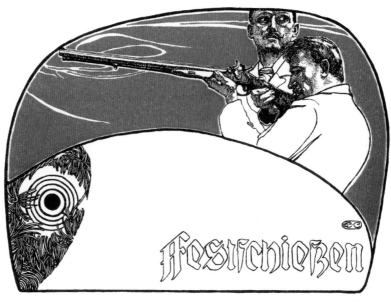

21

22

18

23

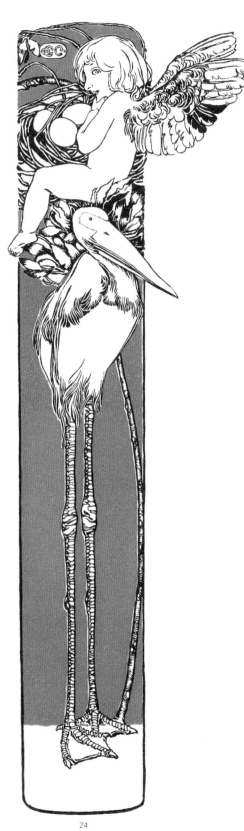

24

25

26

27

28

29

30

31

32

33

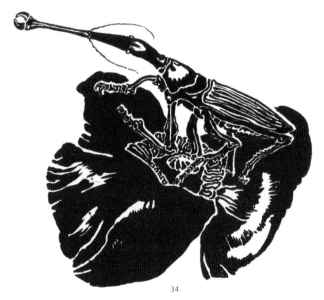

34

35

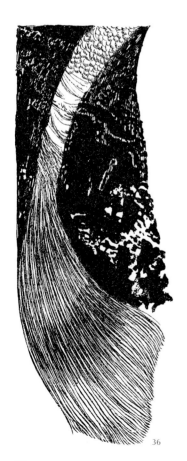

36

37

38

39

40

41

42

43

44

45

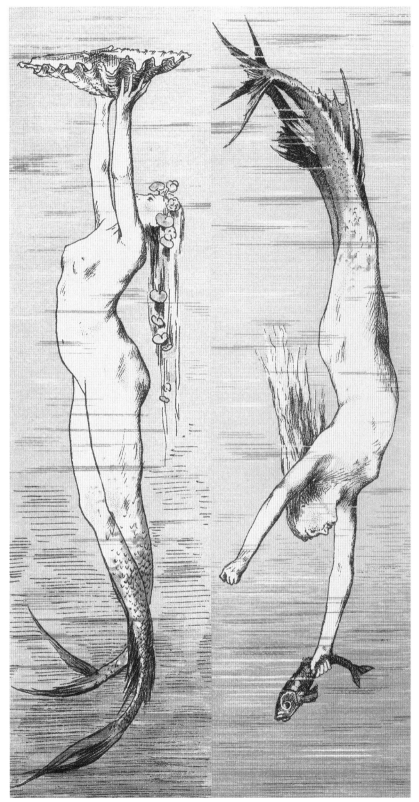

47

48

33

49

50

51

53, 54

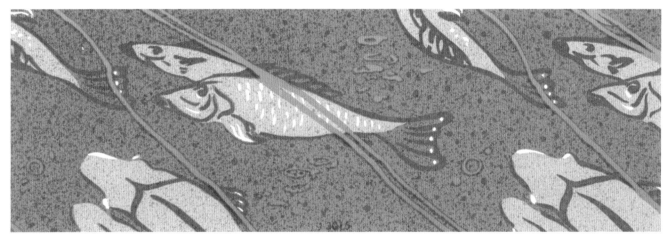

40

58

60

61, 62

64

65, 66

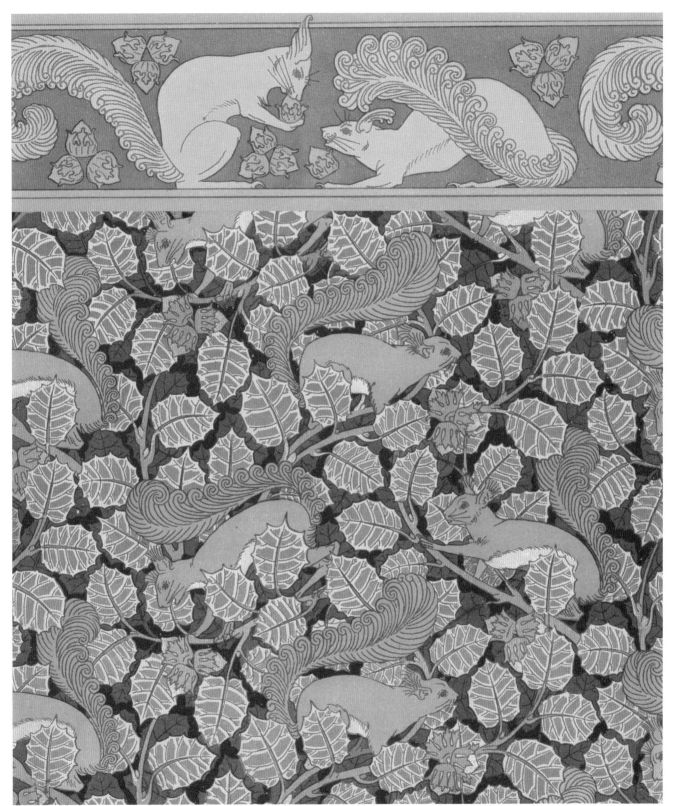

67, 68

69

72

73

74

75

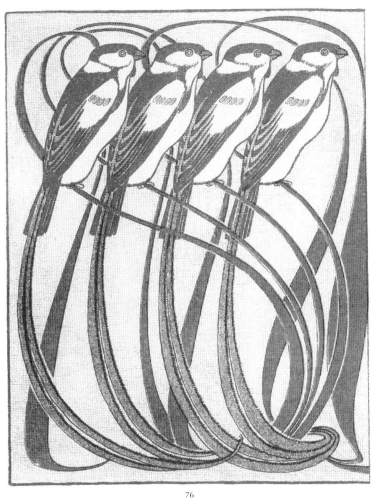

76

78

80

81

82

83

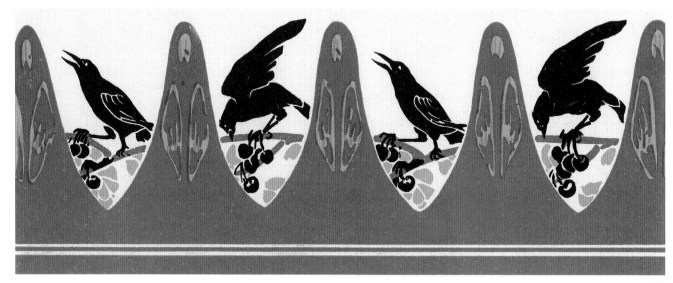

84

85

86

87

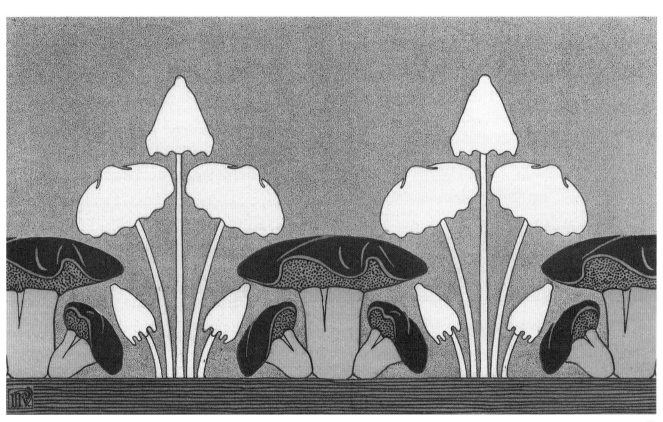

88

89

90

91

92

93

94

95

96

97

98

99

100

101

PLAKAT

ENTWURF
FÜR ABCDEF.

102

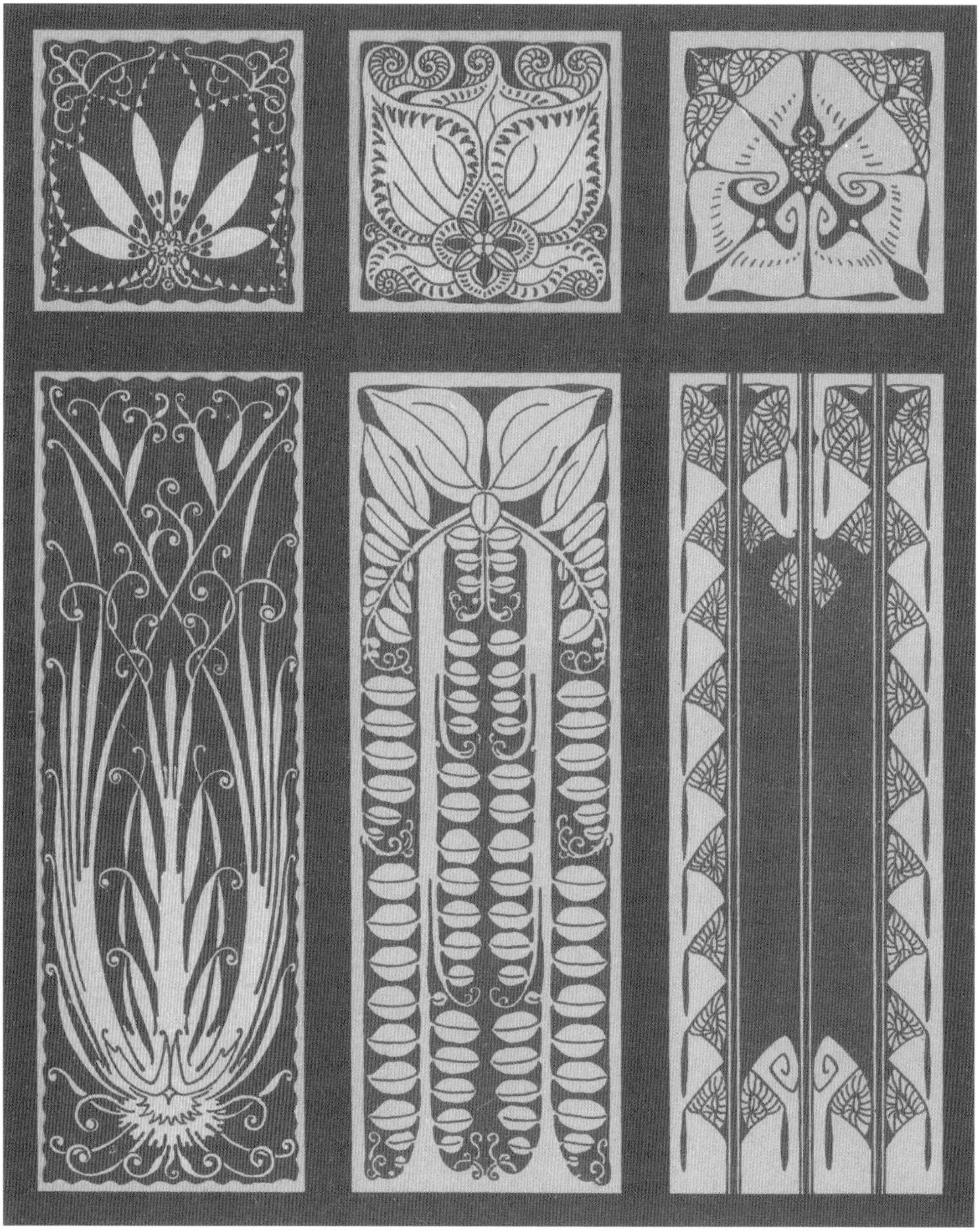

103–105

106–108

109, 110

111, 112

113

114

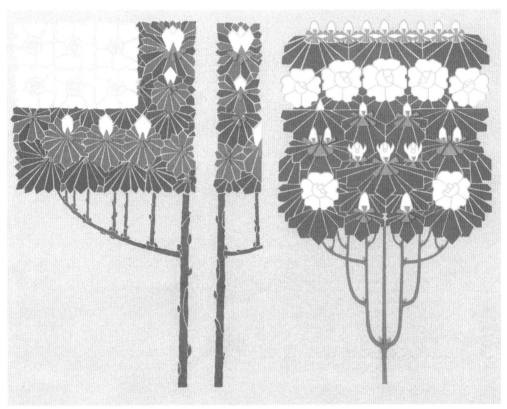

115, 116

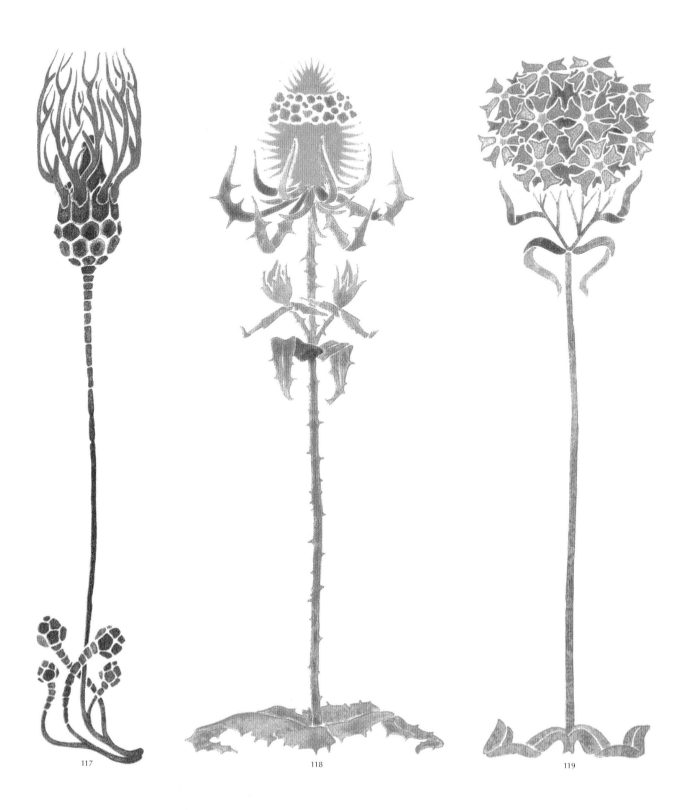

117   118   119

120

121

123

Fragments Floraux

124

125

126

127

129

130

131

274

275

276

277

270

271

272

273

267

268

269

137, 138

135, 136

133, 134

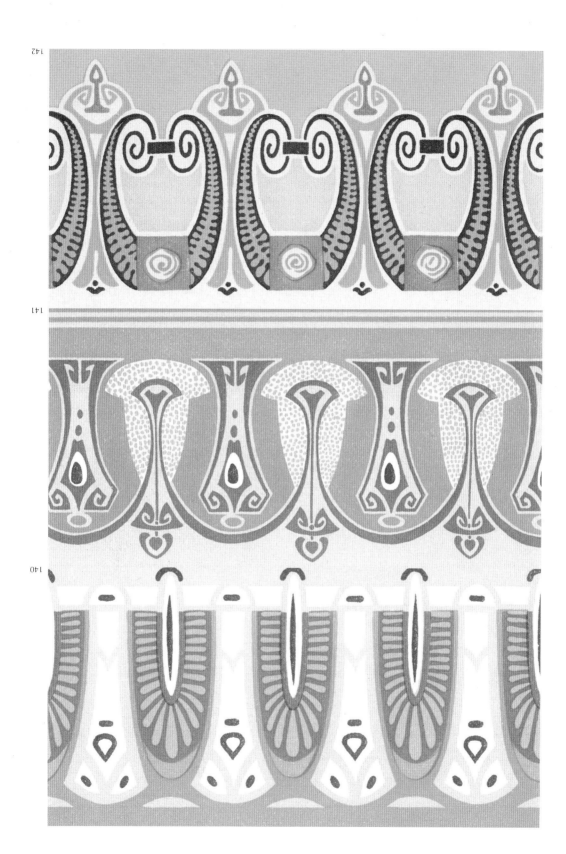

148

147

146

145

144

143

151

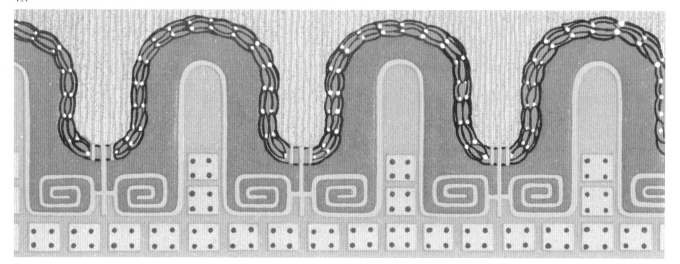

150

149

154

153

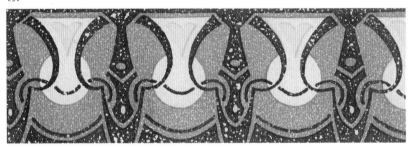

152

157

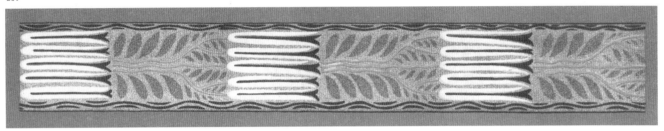

156

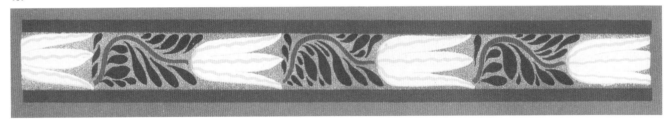

95

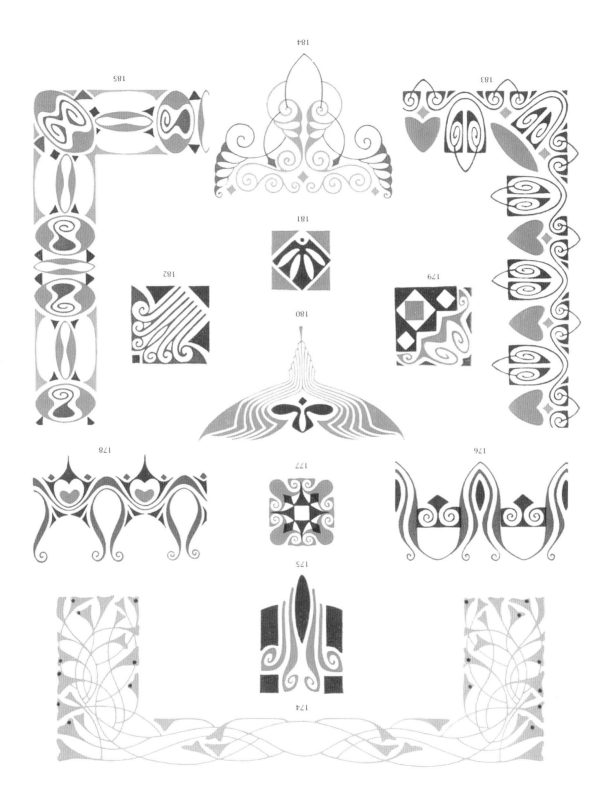

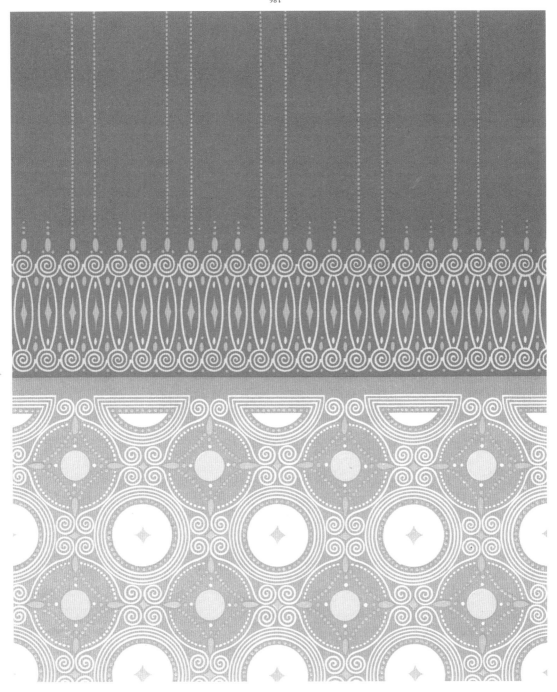

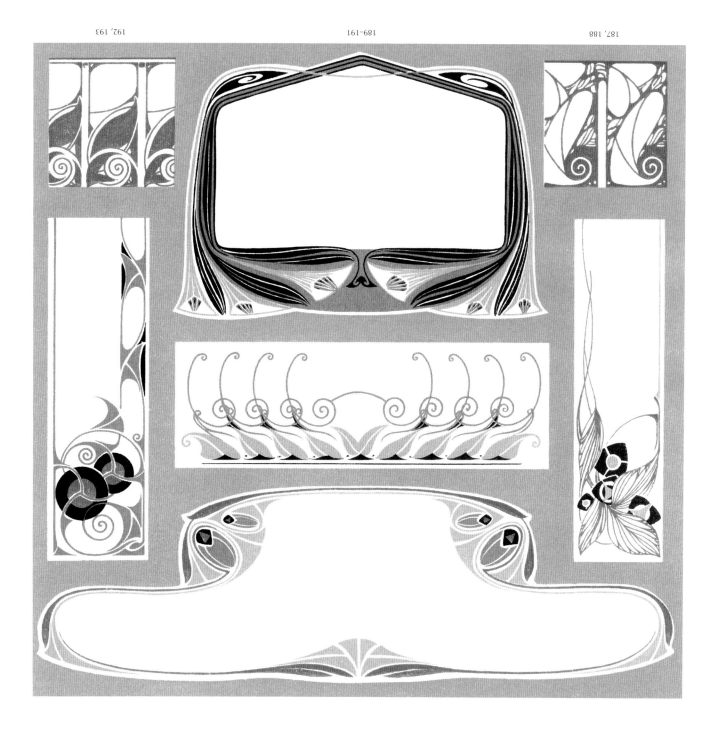

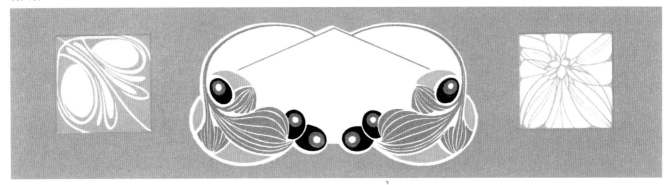

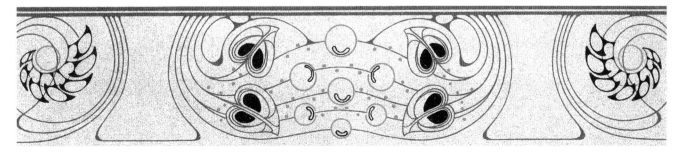

200

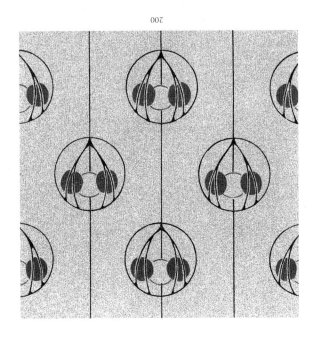

199

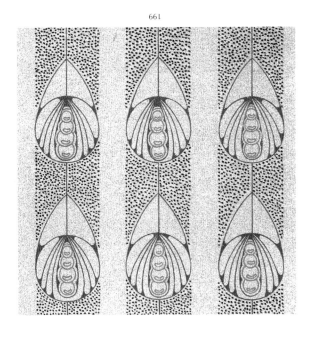

202, 201

203

201, 202

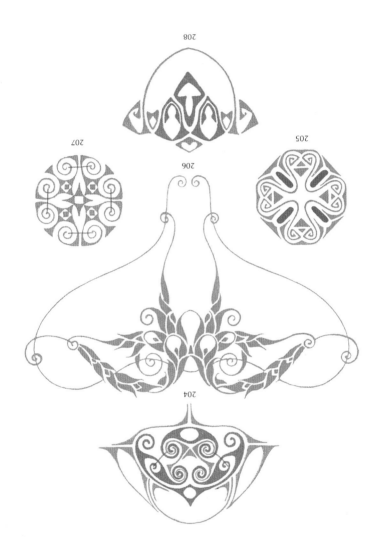

208

207

206

205

204

212-214

217

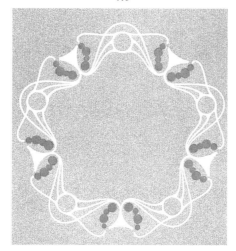

216

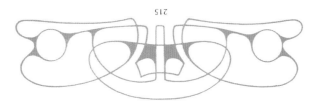

215

218

219

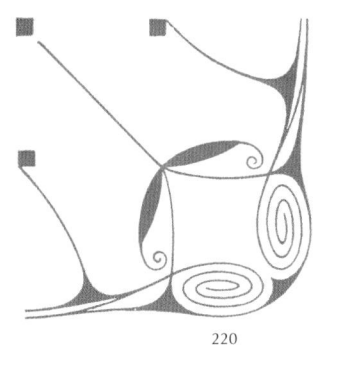

220

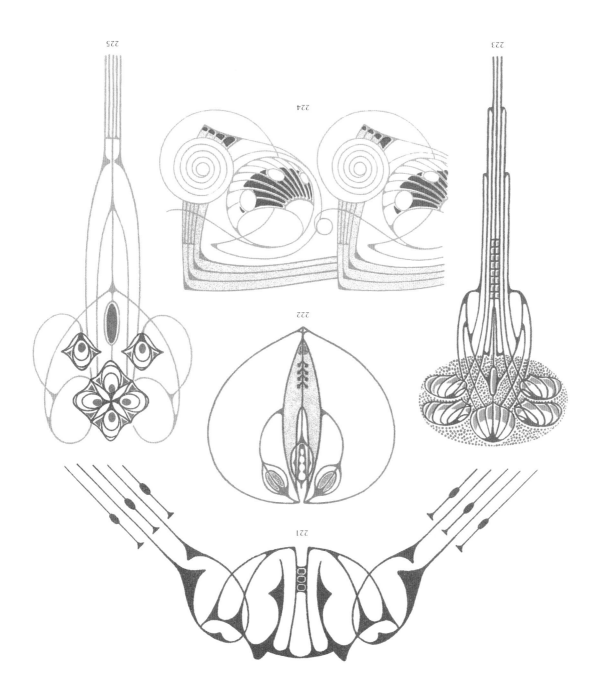

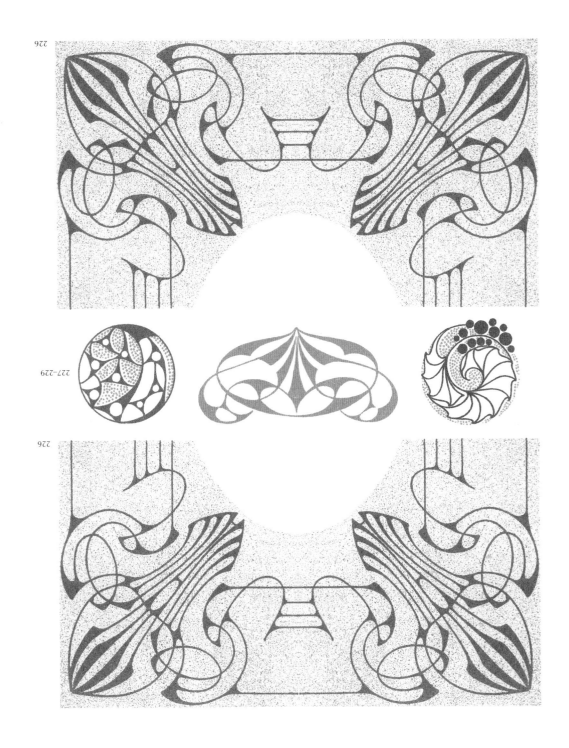

109

226

227-229

226

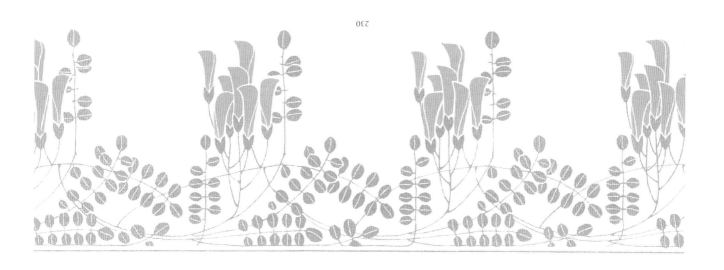

230

235

234

234

236, 237

115

240

245

244

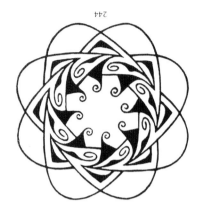

243

242

241

250

252

251

254

253

258

257

256

255

259

260

261

262

266

265

264

263